IMAGES
of America

TYNGSBOROUGH

Captain John Tyng. Captain Tyng was an "Indian fighter" and the son of Colonel Jonathan Tyng, for whom the town of Tyngsborough is named. A Harvard graduate of 1691, Captain Tyng is shown here wearing the scarlet coat of the Massachusetts Militia. In the winter of 1703, he traveled through deep snow to Pequawket (Fryeburg, Maine) to subdue the enemy. In August 1710, he was waylaid and killed, though one source claims he moved to England and died prior to 1721.

IMAGES
of America

TYNGSBOROUGH

Herbert Morton

ARCADIA

First published 1996
Copyright © Herbert Morton, 1996

ISBN 0-7524-0295-1

Published by Arcadia Publishing
an imprint of the Chalford Publishing Corporation
One Washington Center, Dover, New Hampshire 03820
Printed in Great Britain

The River and Railroad. The gentle curve of the Boston & Maine Railroad follows the sweep of the Merrimack River. The familiar arch of the Tyngsborough bridge rests beneath a brooding sky.

Contents

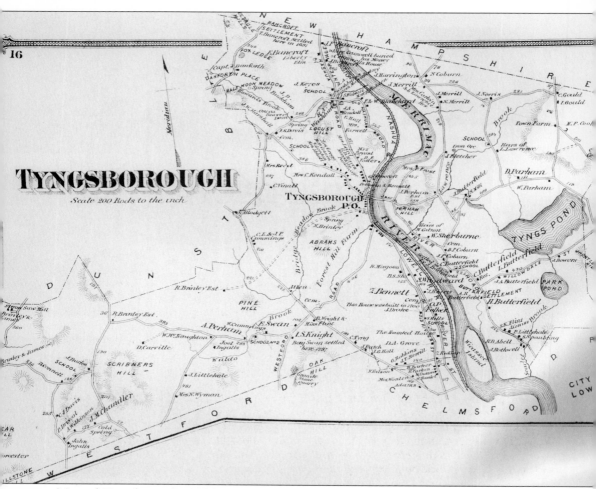

Map of Tyngsborough, 1875. Printed by Middlesex County, this map shows many familiar family names. Note that Flint's Pond was not yet dammed and is shown as Bridge Meadow Brook.

Introduction

It is said that in a small town, everyone knows everyone else. The saying implies the smallness of a town, and the closeness of community. It might be stretched a bit further by saying that in a small town everyone knows everyone else's business, and this might be closer to the truth.

Tyngsborough used to be such a town. To some it might still seem small enough to know everyone, but a look at the names on the tax record for the last forty years will show that the town has grown too fast to keep pace with everyone; much less everyone's business.

While digging up the 194 photographs for this book, I recalled the day when I might have known most of the people in town. Surely, when some of these pictures were taken, the town was small enough so that no one could have escaped the eyes and ears of the rest of the community.

While opinions concerning events and people will change, one thing is constant—change itself. Often, change occurs so slowly that we scarcely notice until it has happened, like the slowly fading rail service to town, or the passing of old town characters who slip away, one by one, until we come to realize they've all gone. At other times, change seems to get up and slap you in the face, such as the redesigning of the center of town to make way for the new bridge, or the dear loss of an historic building, whether by accident or design.

This book contains many old photographs that have been kicking around Tyngsborough for a long time. It was time for the scattered pictures to be gathered together and identified. The research for this book was a welcomed chore, but putting names and dates on each image was not easy. Criss-crossing town with pictures, papers, and notes jotted haphazardly, I dropped in on folks that I visit all too seldom, and gleaned a few names here, a date or two there.

And it came together. I hope readers will enjoy looking back as much as I did. There are faces of people who are known today, and faces of those who were once known, but forgotten. Lost relics of the past, like the Brinley Mansion (p. 51), may cause a person to wonder how many times they passed by, but never stopped. Think of the many "past lives" of the Town Hall, or the gradual expansion of the Winslow School, which grew with the town from the moment of its very beginning.

Remember also that these buildings and others may not be around forever. It is these remaining landmarks that give us our collective character, and give Tyngsborough that something that makes us happy to call this place our home. More should be said of the town's founders, and their characteristic vision and determination. Breaking away from Dunstable, they put together a town that would inspire pride and affection for generations to come.

Herbert Morton
Tyngsborough

One
The Merrimack: Gateway to the North

The Great Curve. The graceful curve of the Merrimack River is shown here in a 1913 photograph taken from the top of Flint's water tower (p. 63). It shows the sweep of the stream as it emerges from Horseshoe Bend on its way to the sea. Above the bridge on the river's western bank a steam train heads north, sending white plumes along behind it.

The Tyngsborough Ferry. The chain ferry was the safest way to cross the Merrimack River before the first bridge was built. Ferry service was started in 1729 by Henry Farwell Jr. In 1809, the county took over the operation during the peak season (April to December), with prices as follows: person on foot, 2¢; person and horse, 6¢; horse and sulky, 17¢; cart and horse, 12 1/2¢; with two horses, 33¢; cart with more than two animals, 40¢; loose animals, 3¢ per beast. Shipping loads were 3¢ per 100 pounds. Passengers pictured here are: Mr. George Danforth (in the bow), Dr. Charles Dutton (holding his horse), and Mr. Ayres Butterfield (the ferryman).

The Henry Farwell Jr. House, 1727. Farwell received his ferry license in 1728. His house overlooking the river was subsequently owned by James Gordon, who operated the grist and sawmills in the center of town, and later by his servant Ovid Houston, who operated a tavern in the house.

A River Cargo Boat. Before the railroad, these boats traveled between Concord, New Hampshire, and the Middlesex Canal in Lowell. They measured 45 to 75 feet long, but were limited in width (9 feet) in order to fit through the locks and canals. They were powered by wind and men with poles, and were towed by steamboat after 1815.

The Boston & Maine Railroad. This steaming locomotive from the early 1930s creates a blur for the camera below the bridge on a cold winter day. Locomotives were a common sight in Tyngsborough Center as they traveled through town to Nashua, Manchester, and points north. Rail service began in 1841.

The *Governor Allen* aground. Not the first to suffer this fate, the *Governor Allen* was one of the last steamers to ply the waters between Lowell and Nashua. The steamers made stops at the Vesper Boat Club in Lowell, Tyng's Island, Harmony Grove, Woodlawn, the Martin Luther Grounds, and the ferry slip and tavern.

The Frost-Snow House, 1733. Once a rendezvous for colonial soldiers and at another time a cobbler shop, this house stands on the corner of Frost and Riverbend Roads. When the town ferry was out of service due to ice, Salathial Frost would bring Dr. Dutton across, rowing from one ice floe to another.

Thompson's Steamer. Running on the river from 1896 to 1909, this steamer boasted a 50-horsepower engine, and could carry two hundred passengers. It made four trips between Lowell and Nashua every Sunday, carrying passengers to Tyngsborough's many outing grounds.

Boardwalk to Steamer. Here we see passengers in the 1890s getting ready to board the steamer. The steamer landing was on the west side of the river near the depot.

Horse Races on the Merrimack. A century ago the river froze solidly from November to March. Sleigh races were held on Sundays. Several racers had fast-steppers, but on the whole, the races were just friendly rivalry. Popcorn and old-fashioned corn cakes with chocolate were sold. The races ended in 1925.

Old Iron Bridge. Opened to the public in the spring of 1874, the old iron bridge was a godsend to travelers weary of the ferry crossing. Originally, it was intended to be set on granite piers atop wooden cribbing, but because of quicksand and river currents, pilings had to be sunk 23 feet below the river's bed. The arches on the eastern side (p. 18) had to be added in 1893 to dampen the sway that had developed. This may have been caused by the dumping of four ox carts of gravel on a single spot of the deck to test the bridge's strength prior to the opening of the bridge.

Merrimack River from Curtis Hill. Taken at the turn of the century from the hill then called Allen's Hill, this photograph shows how much land was once open to pasture, and how grown in it has since become. On the shore of the river in mid-picture is Harmony Grove, a favorite outing ground and steamer stop. On the left the small white cottage in the foreground can still

be seen on the side of Curtis Hill, its paint now gone, its walls crumbling. The white house further away is now a peacefully shaded residence on the corner of Frost Road across from Indian Lane.

The Eastern Entrance to Old Bridge. This shot clearly shows the trusses that were needed to strengthen the eastern half of the iron bridge. Pedestrians cursed the lack of room when two vehicles were passing, causing them to jump up on the narrow side beam or risk bodily injury. A sidewalk was eventually added in 1915.

The Vesper Suspension Bridge. Shown here in 1920, this foot bridge replaced an earlier span which blew down in 1914. The bridge connected Wiccassee (Tyng's) Island with the railroad line across the river. The train was flagged down if anyone wished it to stop. The suspension bridge was dubbed "the longest suspended foot bridge of its width in the world."

The Gangway of the Vesper Suspension Bridge. Looking "up to par" in 1930, the bridge was quite safe, although it was apt to sway in the breeze. It was a favored walkway to enjoy the moonlight during intermission at the dances held by the club. Two or three people swinging in unison was all it took to make the bridge sway—and to give others quite a scare.

The Original Suspension Bridge. In a rare tornado on July 12, 1914, the first Vesper Suspension Bridge was destroyed. It is said that patrons, fearing the bridge might collapse, rushed over the span before it did so, saving them a trip to the center of town. This bridge was built with wooden moorings; the replacement bridge, on the previous page, sported ones made of steel.

The Wiccassee Falls Dam. The remains of the dam that once crossed the river at Tyng's Island are shown here on September 18, 1908, during an exceptionally low river. The building of the Pawtucket Dam in Lowell in 1823 made this dam obsolete. A set of locks operated on the channel side of the island.

Blasting the Dam. During low water, remnants of the Wiccassee Falls Dam were dangerous to river navigation. In 1901, prominent pieces of the remains were dynamited to clear a channel for boats to pass. Parts of the dam can still be seen on the northern side of the island, just south of the power lines.

The Approach to the Old Bridge. The corner of Middlesex Road and the bridge looks bare with the absence of the Adams store, which was destroyed by fire. The old bridge had become shaky and weak; three signs atop one another warn drivers not to exceed 10 mph, as well as admonishing truck drivers not to exceed the posted weight limit of 5 tons.

Ben Lawrence. Making a final crossing of the old bridge in 1932, Ben Lawrence had the distinction of being the first and last to cross the bridge, and the first to cross the new one. The wooden deck of the old bridge rattled from one end to the other.

The New and Old Bridges, 1932. Taken from the First Parish Church, this photograph of both bridges shows the location of the old span. The angle of the older bridge was not noticeable until the new bridge was built in close proximity.

The Two Bridges from the East. On the eastern bank of the river near the entrance to Harmony Grove the two bridges were close together. The old iron bridge, which sat closer to the water, would soon be dismantled. As bridges go, it had a short life—only fifty-eight years.

The Dedication Parade, 1932. Selectmen Homer Noble, Albion Farrow, and Raymond Norton lead a marching band across the old bridge at the dedication festivities of the new bridge. You can see that the deck of the new bridge is somewhat higher than the old one.

The Ribbon-Cutting Ceremony. Homer Noble, A.C. Farrow, and Ray Norton cut the ribbon to open the new bridge to traffic. Pieces of the ribbon were later tied into bows and boxed in display cases. Given only to officials at the time, these boxes are still cherished by their owners today.

Tyngsborough Bridge, 1932. The great sweeping arch of the steel bridge is perhaps the most familiar image in town. It is a focal point for locals and itinerants alike. With its 590-foot span completely out of the water, it seemed to usher Tyngsborough into the modern age. The center of town was completely revamped to accommodate this inspiring edifice, which, until lights were installed in the 1970s, was the longest unlit arch bridge in the Northeast. This shot was taken from the rear of the Hi-Bridge Market now occupied by National Carpets. The high arch frames the familiar buildings of the First Parish Church and Perham & Queen's grocery store.

Spring Flood. In 1936, Tyngsborough experienced its worst flood of this century. Pawtucket Boulevard would be indistinguishable if not for the row of maple trees that once marked its edge. Two men try to make headway against the current—which surprisingly ran north in places, rather than south.

Tyngsborough Station. Stranded in cold water, the depot was abandoned the day before the high water peaked. Traffic was still able to skirt the flood at this time by traveling on Middlesex Road, but Chief Lorman gave Civil Defense Coordinator Chester Queen the alarming news that the water was expected to rise 3 feet per hour before it began to abate.

A Stranded Boxcar. This car contained livestock feed and grain owned by Walter Savill of Dunstable. He removed some grain in the high water, and, thinking it would not get higher, decided to finish unloading the next day. When he came back the following morning, the water had risen to the "NYC" on the side of the car, and his grain was soaked.

Brinley Mansion. Sitting high and dry during the Flood of 1936, the mansion shows the forethought of its builder. The tracks of the Boston & Maine to the left of the guardrails would later end up under 12 feet of water. This was the worst flood since 1897, when similar adverse conditions existed.

High Water. The peak of the flood did not reach the deck of the new bridge, but county officials worried about the foundations. The old bridge, replaced four years earlier, would have been under water. Because of this flood and the ravages it caused, dams were built upstream. We are assured this will never happen again.

Hunter's Barn. This hay barn, owned by Arthur E. Hunter, stood in a field known as the Intervale on Farwell Road. During the Flood of 1936, it was lifted from its moorings and embarked on a river odyssey. The family rushed to the center of town in time to see it crash into the bridge and come apart like a house of cards.

Tyngsborough Depot. After the flood, the high water mark was painted in white on this telegraph pole at the station. No residences were lost in Tyngsborough, but countless buildings from the north floated through town. One building from Plymouth, New Hampshire, started its journey in the Pemigewasset River and settled in a field at the Times Farm in Tyngsborough.

Clearing the Boulevard, April 1936. These men appear to be shoveling snow from Pawtucket Boulevard in front of Charles Coburn's house. However, what they are really shoveling is 3 feet of sand left by the flood that receded a week earlier. This area was under 4 to 5 feet of water.

Two
Industry:
At Home and in Town

The Box Shop from the Water Tower. Looking down from the height of Flint's tower we can see that the box shop and its yard dominated the center of town. The parts of the shop on the left rested where Middlesex Road now passes. The only route north around this sprawling business was Thomas Road, which ran in front of the Winslow School.

The Butterfield Mill. Better known as Sherburne's Saw Mill, the first mention of a mill here is in a deed dated March 31, 1775, when John Perham transferred the property to his son. Butterfield later installed a wool carding machine. In 1923 the mill burned and was rebuilt by brothers Maxwell and Norman Sherburne, who operated it until about 1970.

The Potash Kiln. On Potash Hill, off of Westford Road, this stone fireplace was used to keep embers burning. The embers were used for starting fires when potash was made here for use at the iron foundry in North Chelmsford. The fireplace dates from the 1820s, when the property was sold from the Brinley estate to Major and Mrs. Drake.

The Brinley Stave Mill. This mill and barn was located at the upper dam at Massapoag Pond. Brinley owned a wood road that ran from the farm on Middlesex Road to the pond, parts of which are now Redgate and Cannongate Roads. Though remote today, Massapoag once had a steamboat, dance hall, bowling alley, and picnic groves.

The Oak Hill Quarry. On the southwest side of town on Swan Road, Oak Hill was the largest of many quarries operating in the last century. This picture, mistakenly dated 1800, probably dates from the 1870s. Among the most dangerous of professions, many mining careers were begun and ended here, where work was done with might and brawn, whether by man or ox.

The Adams Store. Here we can examine the store in an early view, before Albert Flint made his improvements. It was built before 1838 by William Adams for his son, and was later taken over by son-in-law Daniel Richardson. Richardson was postmaster and ran a law office upstairs. Deacon Samuel Elliot later ran the store, and is said to have watered his rum down so much that it would freeze. Another tale tells how, during trapping season, he bought muskrat pelts from local boys. Somehow they managed to get them back and sell them to the Deacon again, sometimes three or four times. This store was the location of many heated local and political discussions through the years. It burned down in 1913.

A Flint Ad in the VIA Annual. This 1913 advertisement shows that Flint had other businesses besides making boxes. He owned the Adams store from 1887 until 1904, when the box shop demanded more of his time. He ran the box shop until 1917 when he sold to the Tyng Box Company.

A. A. FLINT

Horseshoeing and blacksmithing of all kinds. Carriage repairing and wheelwright work of all kinds neatly done. Orders solicited for new wagons, dump carts, sleds, and wheelbarrows. I shall carry a good stock of neck yokes, whiffle trees, heel chains and stake chains. When in need of any of the above articles call and get our prices. All work guaranteed. Bring in your farm wagons and second-hand carriages and have them put in first-class repair and painted at once so they will be ready for spring use.

The Horace Washburne House. Washburne operated a brush factory, located at the corner of Middlesex Road and Locust Avenue, from 1875 to 1900. Just after the Civil War, he built a granite dam on Howard's Brook to create Locust Pond on that road. The dam was later rebuilt by Ed Bell in the 1940s. Before Washburne's time, early mill owners relied on two smaller ponds on both sides of Middlesex Road. This corner was once known as Brush Factory Village. Oliver Washburne invented the Washburne dresser brush, which was sold all over the country for more than fifty years. Before the Washburnes, this site was owned by the Holden family (p. 50), who operated a blacksmith shop.

Colonial Hall. The Brinley Mansion, built in 1801, was bought in 1890 by Dr. Orrin Fitzgerald (p. 114), who converted it into a health spa. Fitzgerald spent thousands renovating the house and grounds. An 1893 publicity pamphlet mentions the area's scenic woods, a mineral health spring, and a humbling wooded area called the Four Oaks. The doctor was also a horse-racing enthusiast and ran a breeding farm. His prized possession was the horse Senator Blackburn. Fitzgerald built a racetrack around the front pond at Notre Dame. He also boasted about his setter Rex, "the most educated dog in the world." When he donated a new cupola for the Town Hall to replace the older steeple, townsfolk made up this ditty: "He took the cupola and made it fit; let's give three cheers for Dr. Fitz!"

Perham & Queen's. Perham and a man named Nelson owned the Adams store when it burned, and the two operated out of the barn adjacent to this store for three years. The Perham and Queen partnership began in 1916, when Nelson sold to Chester Queen. Shown here are Adelbert Bell, Enlo Perham, Burt Hodgeman, and Chester Queen.

PERHAM & QUEEN

Dealers in

General Merchandise

Grain, Groceries, Hardware, Paints, Grass Seed, Boots, Rubbers, Fruit and Confectionery.

AGENTS FOR FERTILIZERS and WIRTHMORE GRAIN

TYNGSBOROUGH, MASS.   A NATION-WIDE STORE

A Perham & Queen Advertisement, 1933. This ad for Perham & Queen was seen in many local papers and magazines for close to forty years. Queen tended the store while Perham made pickups and deliveries, taking a different route each day. Their store housed the post office from 1913 to 1958, with Adelbert Bell serving as postmaster.

Ekstrom's Wagon. During the early part of this century, this fine-crafted vehicle was in everyday use at the Ekstrom Farm on Farwell Road. Mrs. Stella (Ekstrom) Beh (p. 82) recalled riding in it with her father to Nashua when Main Street was still unpaved. The wagon is now at the Henry Ford Museum in Dearborn, Michigan.

The Laco Filling Station. This filling station did business in the center near the old bridge. The auto on the left might date this photograph in the 1910s, and the chimney of the box shop in the background gives an idea of the station's location. There were once twenty-six filling stations on Route 3 between Chelmsford and Nashua.

Claude Bell's Fleet. These delivery cars, photographed on a street in Lowell, were Bell's way of getting his patent medicines to town. He and his family manufactured them in their home on Long Pond Road. The cars served well in the city, but Bell cursed the skinny tires each time he had to climb the sandy hill of Long Pond Road on his way home.

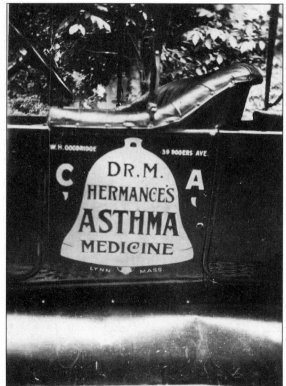

Dr. Hermance's Medicine. A close-up of Bell's logo, taken from an earlier car, advertises his asthma medicine inside a bell. He hailed from Brooklyn, New York, where he purchased the asthma cure from Dr. Hermance. Bell made both tonics and pills for a variety of ailments, making pills upstairs and sending them down to be packaged through a system of chutes.

Marshall Farm. Sisters Anna Sargent and Clara Marshall, with Arthur Marshall beside them, stand on an elm stump in front of their home on Kendall Road. The Marshalls ran a boarding house for summer guests who came from as far away as Rhode Island and New York City. Many guests were recommended to the farm by their doctors for peace and quiet and Clara's noted country cooking. The Carl Gray House across the road was built to handle extra guests when the main house was full.

Nature's Rock Garden. "Come and see the beans baked in the ground!" hawked the sign of this stand on Middlesex Road. "The most unusual roadside stand in the Merrimack Valley" sold milk products, dinners, substantial lunches, gifts, and touted its home cooking, spacious parking, and shaded grove.

Duff's Garage. Fred A. Choate, looking a little like Burt Lancaster, bides his time while waiting to drop off a New Hampshire car he's just towed in to Duff's on Kendall Road in 1938. Is he busy with something, or just camera shy? McCordick's farmhouse stands across the road in the background.

Coburn's Poultry Farm. Johnny Bonzey, Carl Gray, Harold Gilpatrick Jr., Bob Clarke, Harold Wilkins, and Harold Gilpatrick Sr stopped work to pose for this picture in 1935 at the poultry farm on Sherburne Road. The farm was located at the top of the hill across from the apartment complex.

Ty-jayne's Restaurant. Begun as a "fast food" restaurant serving barbecued chicken, this business on the corner of Middlesex Road and Bryant Lane became a family-style restaurant by the late 1950s. The building subsequently served as a pancake house, a teen-age soft drink and dance bar, and finally as a church.

The Tyngsborough Ice Company. Ice harvesting in town was once a flourishing business that was doomed to a slow death. Blocks of ice were harvested by different companies on many area ponds as well as the Merrimack River. Here, on Flint's Pond, workers draw blocks away from a cut with pikes. Frank Sargent operated ice houses here and in Dunstable until his death in 1930, after which they were operated by Henry Desmarias.

An Ice Cutter. This intimidating contraption made the work of cutting ice much faster than it was just a few decades earlier, when horses with scorers and men did the job. The Tyngsborough Ice Company operated until the fall of 1951. Owner Paul Desmarias then conveyed the rights to Flint's Pond and 3 acres of land to the Massachusetts Department of Fisheries and Game, which now controls the level of the pond.

Three
Landmarks:
Natural and Man-Made

Littlefield Library from Flint's Tower, 1913. Middlesex Road, seen on the right, is actually coming from Thomas Road, the present one-way road in front of the Winslow School. Note the two buildings behind the library. The smaller of the two is now a sub shop. The main house was moved back later, when Middlesex was widened.

Tyng Mansion. This was the estate of Jonathan Tyng, for whom Tyngsborough is named. It is thought to have been built before 1675, but 1700 has been offered by former historians. Another early house also built by Tyng lay closer to the river. It was this older house that was also known as the haunted house. The position of the mansion on the side of the hill near the corner of Middlesex and Tyng Roads afforded the Tyngs a grand view up and down the river, and allowed them to keep a watchful eye on Wiccassee (Tyng's) Island, which sits across the river and was the home of some Wamesit Indians who were confined to the island under Tyng's care during King Philip's War.

An Attic Beam in the Tyng Mansion. Harkening back to a dark time in our past, this heavy iron ring was once used for chaining troublesome slaves. The worn spot on the ring's left side shows that it had been used often. Though not universally common or condoned, gentry like the Tyngs often owned indentured servants.

Edward Tyng's Tomb. Dated December 27, 1681, this is the oldest dated burial site in this and many surrounding towns. A brewer in Boston, Edward was the first Tyng to emigrate from England. He secured land grants here for the favor of lending money to the Crown, but did not settle here until his son Jonathan built his home. Note the spelling of the words "LETH," "EDWERD," and "TING."

Tyng's Back Yard. This photograph of the Tyng Mansion shows the working area common with all well-tended estates. Included in this view are the dairy barn, horse stables, carriage sheds, smith shop, servants quarters, and storage sheds. Though refuted, it is said that in 1875, nothing remained of Tyng's earlier home across the street but the cellar hole, as related by historian J.F. Bancroft. The Tyng estate once measured 2,000 acres, stretching from the Chelmsford line to

the center of town, and from the Merrimack River to Massapoag Pond. The Scribner Hill area was known as Tyng's Woods, and rented out to tenant farmers willing to scratch out a living in the rocky soil. This estate was last owned by the Marist brothers, and burned to the ground in 1977.

Map Rock. Located off Old Tyng Road on the former Dunning property, this granite rock bears a depiction of the Merrimack River. It is believed to have been carved by natives in ancient times, but excavations have found no clues. At the top of the rock is the lakes region of New Hampshire, with Horseshoe Bend depicted at the bottom.

The Timothy Bancroft House. The oldest farm in town was established on this site, on Middlesex Road near the New Hampshire line, when Indian trader John Cromwell, the first white man to live in town, set up shop in 1658. The house shown here, built in 1861, replaced an earlier Bancroft home. The location is now the site of the Red Lobster.

The Simon Thompson House. Built before 1728 at the corner of Kendall Road and Locust Avenue, a few town meetings were held here after the state line was drawn in 1741. Before there were any schools, Thompson gathered the neighborhood boys into the barn to "cypher," using the dirt floor for "figgering." It was later known as the Marshall Farm.

Winslow Academy. The school was begun in 1792 with a grant to the town by Madam Sarah (Tyng) Winslow, who also provided funds for the First Parish Church. The grant led to Tyngsborough breaking away from Dunstable as a district in 1789. This is an 1898 pencil drawing; the site is now the rear parking lot for the Shur-Fine Market.

The Nathaniel Holden House, 1799. A veteran of Bunker Hill, Holden built this house at the corner of Middlesex and the northern end of Farwell Road. A farmer/blacksmith, Holden built this ten-room house creatively using wood and iron. Because of his ability to settle disputes he was known as "Peacemaker" Holden.

The William Sherburne House. Built in 1738 by John and Abigail Blood on Sherburne Avenue near Lawndale, this house was purchased by William Sherburne in 1836. The elm tree pictured here once grew in the back yard. William dug it up, carried it through the house, and planted it here. It was the only mature tree in town known to have traveled through a house.

Brinley Mansion. By 1956, what was left of the vast Brinley estate was owned by the Sisters of Notre Dame. After the death of Dr. Fitzgerald, it was owned by famed stage and silent film star Nance O'Neil, who held grand and bawdy parties here. A friend and summer guest was the infamous Lizzie Borden of Fall River.

The Jonathan Kendall House, 1803. Jonathan Kendall was the oldest of three brothers, all carpenters. This is one of only two remaining brick-end homes in town, and is located across Kendall Road from Flint Road. The Kendalls built many buildings in town, most notably the Adams store next to the old bridge and the First Parish Church.

The Jeremiah Kendall House, 1808. This building was built to the east of Jonathan's house by Jeremiah, his second oldest brother. The Kendall family came to Dunstable in 1726, and many branches of the family lived throughout Tyngsborough and Dunstable.

The Moses Kendall House, 1818. Moses, the youngest brother, built this house west of the other two Kendall houses. It is an exact duplicate of his brother Jeremiah's, only the plan is reversed. The brothers were familiarly called John, Jerry, and Mose. A cousin from Dunstable, Amos Kendall, served as postmaster general under President Tyler.

First Parish. This church, erected in 1836, replaced an earlier meetinghouse built in 1755, called the First Parish of Dunstable, which burned in 1835. It sported an ungainly steeple which blew down in the Great Gale of 1815. The need for this church arose in 1741 when the newly drawn state line placed Dunstable's meetinghouse in New Hampshire.

The William Parham House, 1831. When "Squire" Parham built this house, which stands on Coburn Road east of the Lakeview School, Coburn Road did not exist. The actual front of the house faces toward Mascuppic Lake. Parham built the house with bricks made on the property. He served in the War of 1812, and collected a pension during the latter part of his life. He married another Parham, Sarah, and lived here until his death in 1880 at the age of ninety-one, at which time his son John (p. 69) took over the farm.

The Old Mill. Workers at Upton's Box Shop pose over the spillway to the falls. The granite slabs just below the men in the center represent the concrete bridge seen atop the falls in the center of town today. Upton owned property on both sides of the road, including the property where Perham & Queen's would be built. In 1852, Upton leased the area, once a lot for lumber slabs, to Turner and Leird for five years for the sum of 25¢ per year! They brought a building up from Farwell Road and set up a wheelwright shop on the corner. When the lease ran out, Upton moved the building across to his box shop where it became the box shop office.

The Town Farm. In 1835 the old Captain Joseph Butterfield House was purchased by the town as a residence for the needy, who "by circumstances beyond their control" could not support themselves. Before this time, individual farmers with extra room offered bids to care for the poor. In 1826 the first bid was won by Simon Thompson for $414.

The Adams House, 1823. This house was once located on the south side of the First Parish, and was quite small when William Adams built it. About ten years later, Adams hired the Kendall brothers build his store (p. 32). The corner of Winslow Academy (p. 49) can be seen on the far right.

The Adams House, 1869. By this time, the Adams House had grown. A second floor and a farmer's porch were added, along with some fancy trimmings. Many older homes in town have had additions built one atop another, until the building today bears no resemblance to the original.

In its final stage, the Adams House took on another floor and more trimmings. As shown here, it is very different from the modest one-story dwelling that Adams originally built. The Winslow School was moved behind the house and attached to the house's line of carriage sheds.

The Adams House Makes a Move. On September 26, 1973, exactly 150 years after being built, the Adams House was jacked up and moved to Farwell Road. The house traveled up Middlesex Road past Jacoppi's Restaurant and then through the woods to Farwell Road, where it stands today. Winslow Academy, which served for many years as a garage, was moved to Main Street in Dunstable (p. 107), where it was restored by the Tyngsborough-Dunstable Historical Society.

Wannalancet Rock. In 1901, this rock on Tyng Road was dedicated in honor of Wannalancet, chief of the Pawtucket tribe. It was here that he spent his final years in the care of Jonathan Tyng, and pined for his lost heritage. Seen in the center with the medallion is Chief Joseph Laurent of the Abanaki tribe. Historian Jonathan Bancroft stands to the left, and representatives of the Colonial Dames of Massachusetts stand to the right. The inscription reads: "In this place, lived during his last years, and died in 1696 Wannalancet last sachem of the Merrimack River Indians, son of Passaconaway. Like his father, a faithful friend of the early New England Colonists."

Town Hall. All decked out for the Tyngsborough Centennial Celebration in 1909, the Town Hall sports banners, ribbons, and a medallion. Built in 1834 as a Baptist church, it served as such until 1857. The town bought it at auction in 1864. It housed the Winslow School in 1865 and the library in 1878. The cupola was a gift of Dr. Fitzgerald in 1892.

The Evangelical Congregational Church. This handsome church's first communion was held on May 31, 1868. Town residents had the help of three area Evangelical churches in getting the church established. Finding a minister was harder, and the congregation had to offer $1,000 per year for the job. Its large basement was dug by hand in the early 1940s.

The Evangelical Church Interior. This photograph was taken before fixed pews replaced the settees in 1910. The original pipe organ was purchased in June 1898. It was powered by a man in the back room pumping the bellows. The organ was removed when an electric vacuum organ was donated.

The Winslow School. The original school had just two very large rooms when it was built in 1892. In 1915, four rooms were added to the back, and in 1947, four more rooms and offices were constructed. The belfry was replaced with a vent when central heating was installed. At one time, the site was used as a lumberyard for the sawmill in the center of town.

Littlefield Library. Built in 1904, this much-needed library was established with a $5,000 bequest from Lucy Swan Littlefield (p. 70), who asked that the building be named after her daughter Lucy. Before this, the town library was kept in cramped quarters in the Town Hall.

Flint's Water Tower. Albert A. Flint built this water tower for the prevention of fire at his box shop. It stood on the site where the 1958 post office was built (p. 105). The tower had a capacity of 2,500 gallons. In addition to supplying water to the mill, it furnished water to the Town Hall, the Winslow School, and fire hydrants in the center of town.

The Blanchard House. This house on Kendall Road across from the Evangelical church was moved here from Middlesex Road in 1897. Built north of the library, it had to be moved to make way for road widening. Fred Blanchard was station master at the depot for many years, rising at 4 am during winter months to get the fire going.

The Academy of Notre Dame. Nested between the Merrimack River and Flint's Pond, this Catholic school was built on part of the old Brinley estate. The grounds, consisting of 220 acres of water, woods, and hills, were purchased from Nance O'Neil in 1907. The first class of thirty resident students began in 1927.

Massapoag Pond. Tyngsborough's western boundary is shown here from the air in 1948. The boundary marker of Tyngsborough, Dunstable, and Groton lies in the center of the pond, and can be seen by boat under 5 or 6 feet of water. The straight line from left to top is the abandoned Nashua, Acton & Boston Railroad bed.

Four

People:
Windows to Our Past

Gould Cemetery. New roads replacing old ones left this old burying ground out in the woods off of Norris Road. A curious stone, that of Allen Wilson, reads: "He cries no more on Holden's shore, it's witness to his death. For help he cried and sank and died, and water stopped his breath."

"Sir" Robert Brinley. He built the mansion near the First Parish in 1801, the plans for which he took from the Auchmuty House in Roxbury, where he was born. The "Sir" added to his name, and the "Lady" for his wife, were titles ascribed to them by townspeople, not themselves. The Brinleys, like the Tyngs, were considered sympathetic to the Tory cause during the Revolution.

"Lady" Elizabeth Brinley. She was the granddaughter of Judge John Tyng, whose house, built in 1775, stood where the Brinley Mansion was built and burned in the 1790s. Her mother died young and Elizabeth was raised at the local judge's home. Judge John Tyng was the grandson of founder Jonathan. This portrait and the one above were painted by itinerant artist James Bailey Lawson, at a cost of perhaps $20 each.

Dr. Calvin Thomas. Tyngsborough's first town doctor lived in the Farwell House (p. 11). He came to town from Chesterfield, New Hampshire, in 1791, received his MD from Harvard in 1824, and practiced until his death in 1851 at the age of eighty-six. At eighty-four he was still crossing the river by canoe to see patients on the other side.

Ezra Thompson Blodgett. Pausing with his rig on a cold day, he was the son of Deacon William Blodgett, a noted stone mason who worked for many years in the quarries in the western part of town. Deacon Blodgett built the granite wall at the Thompson Cemetery, and that of the Farwell House (p. 11).

Dr. Charles Dutton. In 1868, Dutton became Tyngsborough's town doctor, and was a most beloved servant, tirelessly crossing the river by ferry or other means to see his patients. At times he would travel to Lowell or Nashua to cross: a 12-mile trip. He is best known for his efforts in getting the first bridge built.

John Parham. Descended from one of Tyngsborough's oldest families, John was among the seventh generation of Parhams in this country. He lived in a brick house built by his father (p. 54). His great-grandfather, also named John, was the first white child born on the eastern side of the Merrimack.

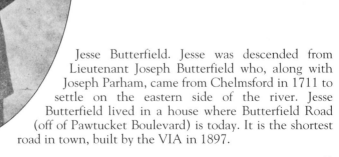

Jesse Butterfield. Jesse was descended from Lieutenant Joseph Butterfield who, along with Joseph Parham, came from Chelmsford in 1711 to settle on the eastern side of the river. Jesse Butterfield lived in a house where Butterfield Road (off of Pawtucket Boulevard) is today. It is the shortest road in town, built by the VIA in 1897.

Lucy Swan Littlefield (1815–1904). It was Mrs. Littlefield's donation which set the building of the Littlefield Library into motion. Her generous $5,000 gift prompted the town to donate $2,500 more to cover construction costs. She died a widow, with all of her children passing on before her.

Lucy Littlefield. The daughter of Lucy Swan Littlefield, she had the new brick library named in her honor. Before her untimely death, Lucy taught school and had the distinction of being one of the first women to be elected to the school committee in 1895.

Jonathan Franklin Bancroft (1847–1925). Bancroft is best known as the town historian, although history and genealogy were only hobbies. A farmer first, with advanced ideas in agriculture, he served on the school board, and helped organize the public library and the Village Improvement Association. Sadly, he never managed to collect his many historical notes into a book, but his collection of historical data is invaluable.

A Winter Carriage. When snow fell, the wheeled baby carriage was stored away and the sleigh carriage taken out. Here, in the winter of 1921, Ethel Clarke pushes her daughter Christina, with son Robert and daughter Frances at her side.

Play Time. Conrad Sargent, sporting a costume and buggy in 1909, plays across the road from his aunt's home at the Marshall Farm (p. 39). It was customary for children to spend weeks or months away from their Dunstable homes in the summer, not to give parents a rest, but to offer older relatives some free help with chores.

River Ice. An afternoon shadow is all that can be seen here of George Robeson (p. 125) as he takes a picture of high ice on the river in 1936. Ice blockages pushed up onto the railroad tracks at times, and they needed to be cleared by hand to allow trains to pass.

Conrad Sargent (1903–1983). Except for a few years with the police department (p. 96), Mr. Sargent was self-employed throughout most of his life in Tyngsborough. He began work for his father Frank who dealt in ice, lumber, and construction. Conrad recalled ten-day trips walking cattle down to town from a family farm in Bath, New Hampshire.

Claude and Edith Bell. In addition to his patent medicines (p. 38), Bell was one of the first in town to have electricity in his home. He generated his own in the cellar with a gasoline motor, storing it in banks of glass batteries. This power supply then ran to a single light in each room of the house.

Arthur (Ren) Marshall (1859–1955). Marshall was born and lived out his life on the family farm on Kendall Road. Tall, thin, and erect well into his nineties, he was as much a character at town meetings as his face implies in this photograph. His only position other than being a farmer was that of highway surveyor in the 1920s.

The Ladies Social Circle. At an all-day meeting *c.* 1920 at Clara Parrish's house, the social circle began with the Evangelical Church. They didn't wish younger members to join; the Evangelical Women's Club was begun for the younger crowd. Later, when only a few members of the Social Circle remained, they joined the Women's Club. Pictured here are, from left to right: (front row) Miriam Robeson, unknown, Mrs. Brown, and Edith Connell; (back row) Clara Parrish, Agnes Keyes, Dorothy McLoon, Lottie Haley, unknown, Mrs. Nelson, unknown, Maude Currier, Gertie Connell, Francena Sherburne, and Mary Robeson.

A Brownie Troop. Ruth Wilkins and Bessie Norris were troop leaders in this picture dated June 6, 1932. Pictured are, from left to right: (front row) Gladys Cobleigh, Esther Sherburne, Avis Bell, and Margaret Coburn; (back row) Dorothy Lowe, Ruth Hall, Miriam Wilkins, Muriel Cobleigh, Rita LeBlanc, Louise Clarke, Doris Ford, and Dorothy Cobleigh.

Perham & Queen. Copying an earlier picture (p. 36), George Bell, postmaster Adelbert Bell, Chester Queen, and Enlo Perham stand in front of the store in 1946. George Bell and brother-in-law Bill Farrow took over Perham & Queen's in 1946, running the store until 1960 when Farrow took sole ownership.

Bessie Norris (1892–1976). Norris taught at the Winslow School from 1916 until she retired in 1961. During part of that time she also served as the school principal. Seen here in 1932, she was active in the Girl Scouts. She also held membership in the First Parish, Ladies Alliance, the historical society, and the VIA.

Charles A. Lorman. Appointed chief of police in 1935, Lorman served in that capacity until his retirement in 1952. In his first year, radio communication was installed for the first time, in his private car. It was a one-way radio, allowing incoming calls only, and was connected with the Nashua Police Department.

Ethel (Cheney) Sargent. Standing at her son's home on Kendall Road in 1948, Mrs. Sargent was a founding member of the Tyngsborough-Dunstable Historical Society. She also held positions in the Evangelical Women's Club and Tyngsborough Grange #222.

John Barr. For many years, Mr. Barr worked in the passenger rail service, but it was Tyngsborough's trolley service on both sides of the river that held his interest. His father operated a large apple orchard on Norris Road. John donated the Gould Cemetery to the town in the 1970s.

Mrs. Wiley's Second Grade, 1949. The class stands on the front steps of the Winslow School. Pictured are, from left to right: (front row) Priscilla Cabana, Priscilla Lorrey, Phyllis Parlee, Lee Betz, Carol Marinel, Carolyn Jordan, Suzanne LeBlanc, Barbara Bosse, Simone Bergeron, and Evelyn Price; (second row) Dora Mae Gotham, Sandra Wilkins, Alice Smith, Carol Gilinson, Janice Landry, Doris Chaput, Judith Saunders, Ramona Morton, and Pauline Ouelette; (third row) Thomas Coyle, James Choate, David Allen, Louis Courtemanche, Robert Gray, Donald McPhee, Robert Brick, Roger Soulard, Donald Carkin, Ronald Hoyt, and Bill Landry; (back row) Bill Faulkner, Richard Lustig, Dennis LeBlanc, Albert Johnson, Albert Chounard, George Toy, Dennis Gagnon, Roy LeMasurier, Stephen Ames, and Manuel Gray.

Perambulating the Bounds. Town officials of Tyngsborough, Groton, and Westford are shown storing energy for the next phase of walking the boundaries of town in 1956. According to historic state laws, it is mandatory that at least two selectmen from each town walk and mark the bounds every five years, lest the town forfeit $20. This was not an easy task because one boundary rests in the middle of Massapoag Pond (p. 64). Seated are Fire Chief Robert May and Harold Barber of Groton. Seated behind them are Carroll Rollins of Westford, Tyngsborough Selectmen John Lewis, and Albert Holdsworth. In the back are Thomas Park of Groton and Horace Wyman of Westford.

Charles Derbabian (1904–1983). Charlie was the janitor at the Winslow School for many years. Generations of school kids, as well as countless residents, became friends with him, admiring both his jovial spirit and no-nonsense attitude. He emigrated from Armenia with his parents and brother in 1909.

The Tyngsborough-Dunstable Historical Society. The organization was started in 1939. Pictured here in 1958 are: Lena Coburn, Barbara Hammond, Chester Queen, Bessie Norris, Louis Spindell, Mrs. Louis Spindell, and Catherine Lambert. Mrs. Lambert is best remembered for her enthusiasm in her efforts in documenting much of our history.

Robert Duff. Bob was appointed fire chief in 1951. He operated Duff's Garage on Kendall Road across from the highway department until he retired in 1978. The business was started by his father George, who built the town's first fire truck (p. 95).

The Ekstrom Farm. Stella (Ekstrom) Beh and her brother, John Ekstrom, stand in Stella's kitchen at their family home on Farwell Road. John ran his own farm up the road from 1929 until he retired (it is now Parlee's Farm). Stella spent many years as a nurse, returning to country life after she retired.

Five
Around Town:
Scenes and Events

Winslow in Winter. In yet another view from Flint's water tower, the snow-covered Winslow School grounds lie before the many houses along Kendall Road (left). Far away to the west on the horizon are the hills of Dunstable.

The Westford Road Schoolhouse. Schoolhouse No. 2 served "all of the First Parish on the westerly side of the Merrimack, excepting Lieut. Perham and Mr. John Bridge." From left to right are: George W. Merrill, Charles E. Glidden, Lizzie Smith, Emma Carville, Serena Perham, and the teacher, Miss Georgia May Cummings.

Electric Cars. Trolley service to Tyngsborough village from Lowell began in 1897 and continued until the early 1930s. Across the river, Lakeview Avenue (between Lake Mascuppic and Frost Road) was built as a trolley line in 1895, and was utilized until 1924. Lakeview Avenue was originally a service road for the tracks, and became a road later.

Grades Five and Six, 1904. At the new Winslow School building, this class photograph shows how the large rooms looked before the major improvements occurred with the 1915 addition. These two grades only take up three rows of a classroom that held eight rows of desks. Advanced classes held at the original Winslow Academy would soon come to an end. Only three children are identified here: "Charles Coburn, dark jacket middle row; Avis Blodgett, first in last row; and Hazel Hodgeman, behind her."

Looking Down Kendall Road into the Tyngsborough Square *c.* 1920. The Town Hall and two houses on the right are the only remaining buildings. At the far left is the peak of the old box shop. Straight down the road in the distance is the Adams store, with the Laco Filling Station to the left of it. To the left of the store, hidden behind the filling station, lies the entrance to the old bridge.

Tyngsborough Square, A Decade Later. With the building of the new bridge, the small village was cleared away and thousands of yards of fill had to be brought in to allow Middlesex Road to run straight through. The fill was hauled in from behind the home of Sylvia Pelletier on Kendall Road, where the northbound ramp to Route 3 is today. A concrete culvert was poured below the dam and falls and the great gully was filled. One plan was to have an overpass, where traffic from the bridge and Kendall Road would pass underneath Middlesex Road, with ramps connecting the two. After much heated debate, the intersection plan was decided on, which spawned grudges that would last for years.

Tyngsborough Square. In this *c.* 1920 view, from the entrance to the old bridge, Perham & Queen's seems small compared with the store today. The large white building in the center became the Laco Filling Station (p. 37). This postcard was issued by Perham & Queen's. Hundreds of these cards were thrown out during renovations.

Tyngsborough Square. Adding the First Parish Church to the picture provides some bearing for those too young to remember the changes. The towering box shop chimney was put up in 1893 and considered a marvel to folks who had never been out of town. One July Fourth, some men hoisted a four-wheeled dump cart to the chimney top. No one knew how they did it, but it was a chore getting it down.

Main St., Tyngsboro, Mass.

Town Common. Looking south from the square, with the Adams store on the left, a trolley car approaches from North Chelmsford. The lush growth of elms on the common hangs nearly over Main Street (Middlesex Road). In the distance behind the trolley rests the train depot. A trolley ride from Lowell cost 10¢ and took about forty-five minutes. In 1897, when the first trolley came to town on this line, the event was celebrated by a cannon shot from the grounds of the Merrill House, where Winterwood Store is today. The shot did not hit the trolley, but the percussion of the blast shattered all the windows in the street car.

Flint's Pond. This large pond, now controlled by the Massachusetts Department of Fisheries and Game, was the natural stream bed of Bridge Meadow Brook. It was dammed up after 1875 to provide a back-up water supply for the box shop. Potash Hill is on the far left, with Abrams Hill just to the right of it. Skirting these hills near the edge of the pond was the Brinley Wood Road that led from the Brinley farm to Massapoag Pond. The Henry Farwell Jr. House on the bottom right shows the low slope of its northern roof. Many early homes offered such a roof to combat the cold and wind from the north, while utilizing two floors of windowed walls to the south.

A Gristmill Stone. This stone, dug up on the site of the former box shop, was used at William Gordon's gristmill, and was recently set into the front lawn of the Town Hall. There were two sets of these granite stones, and perhaps three more are still buried at the site.

Bridge and Old Post Office, Tyngsboro, Mass.

The Old Bridge and Post Office. By 1898, Flint had finished improving the Adams store (p. 32). He moved the store closer to the river and added on a new front. With three dormers added to the third floor, this space was made into living quarters. Flint sold the store to Nelson & Perham in 1904.

The Centennial Celebration, 1909. Reverend James Danforth, Otis L. Wright, and Wallace P. Butterfield formed the general committee to organize Tyngsborough's 100th birthday. The celebration began Sunday, June 27, 1909, and lasted three days. Opening-day services were held at the First Parish. Monday was Winslow School alumni day, with a rededication of the original Winslow School bell, a banquet and meeting, followed by a two-hour steamer ride on the river. Later that night, French's orchestra from Nashua played at the Town Hall. Tuesday saw a concert at a decorated bandstand at the Winslow School, given by the Waltham Watch Company Band. A banquet was followed by another concert, and a grand ball at the Town Hall finally topped off the three-day event.

James Burrows. An eloquent and fascinating orator, Burrows spoke on the last day of the Tyngsborough Centennial Celebration. Though from Lynn, he was born in Tyngsborough and recalled his first images of the river. He was introduced as having "wandered far and wide since leaving, from the Atlantic to the Pacific, and even across the ocean."

Scouts, Troop #1, 1933. With eleven new members, troop #1 had thirty-two scouts and three associate members. Their meetings at the Town Hall included classes, singing, games, and dancing. Lieutenant Catherine Collier and Lieutenant Francis Savill of Dunstable are the leaders shown here.

A Spring Freshet, 1932. By this time the dam and falls were all that remained of the once-thriving box shop and mill. Spring run-off filled the spillway. Trees had not yet taken over, and everything still appears new after the recent construction.

A Spring Freshet, 1950. In the same location, eighteen years later, willow trees have grown tall and lush. Standing in among these trees made a person feel as if the area was larger than it really was; a stranger would have no idea how much the terrain had changed.

The New Tyngsborough Fire Station, 1932. Chief Harold Dunlap stands before the fleet. The truck on the right was Tyngsborough's first fire truck, built from scratch by George Duff. It sports the old ferry bell that once alerted passengers that the ferry was about to leave. The truck on the left was "store bought."

A Fire Engine, c. 1935. Some years later, an early fire truck pulls out of its berth at the station. The engine was small, but state-of-the-art, for 1930s Tyngsborough. Drivers had to deal with the elements. "Babe" Boucher in front of the truck looks on as Perley Knight checks behind the seat.

The Town Marker. An unidentified friend of Edith Bell poses next to the cornerstone marking the convergence of three towns: Tyngsborough, Hudson, and Pelham (New Hampshire). A smaller marker, found on the side of Sherburne Road in Hudson, points into the woods where this marker is found.

Police Officers, 1938. Four police officers stand in the driveway of the Town Hall. Police headquarters were in the basement of the building where town offices are located today. From left to right are: Jack Riley, Chief Charles Lorman, Conrad Sargent, and Herb Riley.

Tyngsborough's First Dialed Call, 1939. Selectman Homer Noble places the first dialed telephone call from his office in the Town Hall to his home on Farwell Road, August 17, 1939. Before this time all calls were routed through an operator at the Davis home (Farwell House, p. 11).

The Telephone Exchange Building. Located on the corner of Kendall and Flint Roads, this small building housed the newfangled contraptions that made dialed calls possible. The building has grown quite a bit since 1939. The first operator telephone exchange in 1905 was near the corner of Kendall Road and Locust Avenue in the present Richardson home.

TYNGSBOROUGH — MASSACHUSETTS

TOWN OF TYNGSBOROUGH MASS.

HONOR ROLL

CARL D. ALLGROVE
WARREN W. ALLGROVE
MARGARET J. BANCROFT
RAYMOND BARLOW
ROLAND E. BELL
WENDELL BLANCHARD
CHARLES E. BROCK JR.
LAWRENCE E. BROWN
WALLACE C. BUTTERFIELD
ARTHUR H. CABANA
BERNARD L. CABANA
FREDERICK M. CARTER
WILLIAM A. CARTER
ORVILLE F. CHUBB
HORACE O. CLARKE JR.
HARRY R. CLARKE
PAUL J. CLARKE
FRANK E. COBLEIGH JR.
WILLIAM H. COCORAN
JOHN F. CONLON
LOUIS R. COTE
FRANCIS D. CRYAN
THOMAS CRYAN
CHARLES H. CURRIER
FRANK DEFOE
NORMAN A. DEMARRIS
PAUL DEMEDEROS
ELMER D. DODGE JR.
JEAN R. DUBE
RAYMOND K. DUNNING

ERNEST R. DUPRAS
RICHARD W. DUPRAS
WARREN W. FABYAN
WENDELL N. FABYAN
HOWARD W. FAY
WILLIAM C. FLANAGAN
E. PRESCOTT FORD
WALTER H. FRYE
EDWARD GAUDETTE
JOSEPH L. GERVAIS
JOSEPH R. OUILLAGE
ELBERT A. HALEY
HARRY C. HARDING
RUSSELL O. HUGHES
STANLEY A. JANKOWSKI
KENNETH C. JORDAN
WM. SUMNER KENNEY
LUCIEN A. LACOURSE
GERALD J. LAMBERT
CURLISS B. LAMBERT
DAVID LAMBERT
RICHARD H. LAMBERT
ROBERT D. LAMBERT
HOWARD E. LANGLEY
JOSEPH N. LANGLOIS
LEO N. LANGLOIS
PAUL J. LEAVER
ERVIN M. LEONARD
OTIS L. LEONARD
FRANCIS W. LOVERING

CHARLES T. MARINEL
FRED M. MARLOWE
JAMES P. MARLOWE
ROBERT J. McCARTHY
EMERY W. NOLET
WILLIAM S. NOWELL
JOHN N. ONEILL
HENRY A. PELLETIER
DOUGLAS C. PELLETIER
JOSEPH B. PELLETIER
RALPH N. PELLETIER
ROBERT D. PELLETIER
HAROLD PETERS
WILLIAM J. PORTEAS
KENNETH H. PORTER
RAYMOND A. RADICOT
CLAYTON H. REED
MENDALL A. REED
ROBERT R. REED
RUSSELL E. ROBERTS
RALPH C. ROBESON
ELLIOT SCIMEMI
FRANK SCIMEMI
WARREN L. SHEPHERD
ARTHUR E. SHERBURNE
RUSSELL K. SHEABURNE
HAROLD L. SIMPSON
RALPH E. SIMPSON
GEORGE R. SINGLETON

RICHARD A. SINGLETON
ARTHUR F. SMITH
DAVID H. SMITH
CHARLES L. STEPHENSON
RICHARD B. STEPHENSON
GLENN STEVENS
EARLE R. STRATTON JR.
HARRY L. SWAN
LIONEL B. TFYREAULT
JOSEPH D. THIBAULT
ALBERT J. TRIPANIER
EDWARD E. URBANOWICZ
ISADORE VAUCOURT
ARMAND E. VIGNEAULT
CHARLES L. WEBSTER
HARLAND P. WIGDON
CRAIG D. WILBUR
GLENN L. WILBUR
WAYNE A. WILBUR
HAROLD B. WILLIAMS JR.
RAYMOND M. WILKINS
HARRY S. WINER
FRANK A. WYMAN JR.
WHITNEY K. WYMAN
KAREKIN H. ZEMANIAN
THERESA M. BARNETT
ARTHUR B. BELL
GEORGE A. BELL
THEODORE E. BOUCHER JR.
FRANCIS N. CARTER

JEAN D. COTE
GERALD CRYAN
ROBERT P. DeCARTERET
LAWRENCE A. DELISLE
ROBERT O. DUFF
GEORGE FORD
RAYMOND E. FOREST
ALFRED FRANCOUR
SAMUEL L. FULLER
L. GEORGE GAUDETTE
CLIFFORD E. JORDAN
ROSARIO L. LACOURSE
EILEEN C. ONEIL
HERBERT E. RILEY
WALTER F. SHAW
KENNETH L. SINGLETON
SHIRLEY C. WYMAN
JAMES M. CARTER
MAURICE H. COBLEIGH
MAURICE L. COYLE
CLAYTON F. CROSBY
ROBERT DESMARAIS
ROLAND DERBY
PAUL A. EKSTROM
NATALIE FARROW
JAMES FUHRMAN JR.
ALFRED O. GOSSELIN
CURTIS A. GUILD
HENRY J. LAFRANCE JR.
OMER LACOURSE

CHARLES A. LORMAN
RUSSELL A. LEONARD
HAROLD C. MALLOY
GEORGE A. McCARTHY
JOSEPH A. PELLETIER
RAYMOND PICARD
OLIVER A. ROBINSON
ARTHUR L. SMITH
THOMAS L. WALKER
CHARLES H. COOPER
WESLEY H. DAVIS JR.
BURTON K. DODGE
WILBER C. FABROW
FREDERICK P. FLANAGAN
BOWERS FULLER
LEO F. FLANNAGAN
RALPH GOODWIN
RALPH L. JORDAN
LEO A. LORD
EDWARD A.D. MOSS 3rd
WILLIAM S. MARRIOTT
HARVEY E. PINEO JR.
RICHARD A. STEVENS

Honor Roll. This monument was erected on the lawn between the Winslow School and the Littlefield Library to honor townspeople who served in the armed services during World War II. It appears to be of stone but was actually made of wood. It blew down during a hurricane. A permanent monument across the road on the common replaced it (p. 104).

The Highway Department, c. 1944. George Ford, and Leo and Joe Pelletier stand beside a 1937 vintage truck at the town sheds. Leo was highway surveyor from 1942 until his death at age eighty-four. It is said he could load a truck with a shovel faster than two other men.

The Town Sheds. Until 1966, the highway department and the fire department were housed directly behind the First Parish. The garage, seen on the far left and attached to the Adams House, is the former Winslow Academy (p. 49).

The Fire Department. In this front view of the town sheds we can see the fire department occupying the left half of the building. The upstairs room was used for meetings from 1932 until the mid-1950s. A siren on the roof sounded each evening at seven o'clock. The siren was sounded by a button in the Sherburne home. If the Sherburnes were away, Mrs. Sargent took over.

Tyngsborough Station. Mrs. Whalen, who lived in the Bennett-Perham House at the corner of Westford Road, greets State Representative Edith Nourse Rogers c. 1949. A decade later, the depot was gone but the train still stopped for passengers at the siding.

Saturday Morning at the Depot. On a typical morning, workers and shoppers waited at the station for their ride into Lowell and points south. Up the tracks, the train can be seen slowing down for a stop. When the depot was gone, a freight platform was all that remained. By 1970, the train no longer stopped.

The Tyngsborough Volunteer Fire Department. Shown are members of the first graduating class of trained firemen, November 27, 1950. Trained in fire fighting and safety, this class was certified the same year that Station 2 was built. The station was constructed on Lakeview Avenue on property donated by Leo Flanagan. From left to right are: (front row) Chief Guy Constantine, Frederick Flanagan, Assistant Chief Arthur (Ski) Bell, Harold Bell, William Bell, Lucien Bergeron, and Leo Castonguay; (middle row) Wilfred P. Mercier, Leo Flanagan, Leo Bergeron, Robert Dingle, James Dingle, Richard Coughlin, Dr. Raymond Chouinard, and Theodore (Ed) Coughlin; (back row) L. Roger Castonguay, Charles R. Waldrep, Richard Singleton Sr., Frederick Shanahan, Romey Shanahan, Ben Rondo, Donald Rand, and Raymond (Chuck) Piccard.

Leo G. Pelletier, *c.* 1955. While employed as a highway surveyor, Leo stands beside Tyngsborough's new road grader. George Gaudette, seen in the cab, operated the grader for many years. His worst experience at the job came while widening Westford Road, where he tangled up with poison ivy, and landed in bed for a week.

The Tyngsborough Sportsmen's Club. Begun in 1938 and incorporated in 1942, the club's meetings were held in private homes until the first clubhouse was built in 1945 on Westford Road. This newer building was built in 1959. The trout pool dug in 1956 is considered one of the best in New England.

A *Boston Post* Cane. Once passed down in turn to the town's oldest resident, canes were given to 431 towns in five states by Edwin A. Grozier, editor of the *Boston Post*. In 1909, the gold-topped ebony canes were handed out as a publicity gimmick to boost the paper's circulation. Today, the cane rests in the vault of the Town Hall.

Miss Cannon's First Grade. Santa Claus made his annual visit to this class at the Winslow School in 1956. The excess facial hair kept the six-year-olds from recognizing the school's custodian, Charles Derbabian (p. 81). Charlie made these seasonal rounds to all the lower grades.

The Veteran's Monument Dedication, June 5, 1955. This granite marker honors Tyngsborough veterans who served and paid the supreme sacrifice during World Wars I, II, and the Korean conflict. The monument replaced the temporary marker (p. 98) that was destroyed by Hurricane Edna. The ceremony drew five hundred spectators. The National Anthem was played by the thirty-piece 18th Army Band from Fort Devons, and was followed by a dedicatory address by Congresswoman Edith Nourse Rogers. Standing before the monument are three Gold Star mothers: Mrs. Preston H. Fay Sr., Mrs. Wesley H. Davis Sr., and Mrs. Leo G. Pelletier.

The U.S. Post Office, 1958. This view shows the dedication of the new post office at the corner of Middlesex and Farwell Roads. This was the first time Tyngsborough's post office had its own building. The office was formerly at Perham & Queen's store from 1913 to 1957, and at the Adams store prior to that.

The Tyngsborough Police Department, 1959. Shown are, from left to right: (front row) Joe Reedy, Mike Kilowski, Chief Harold Pivirotto, George Newell, and Clarence Cody; (back row) Charles Lynch, Paul Fazel, Arthur (Ski) Bell, Mitt Estabrook, and Harold Newcomb.

The Brinley Crypt. Actually the crypt of Judge John Tyng, this crypt predated the Brinley Mansion. It was all that remained of the Judge's house after the 1800 fire. Left to disrepair after the Brinleys were gone, it was a curiosity for local children. It was restored by Ted Zeibrick after being neglected for years with little more than a board for a cover.

Inside the Crypt. Gypsum can be seen leaching through the old hand-made bricks. Meant to be sealed whenever a tier was filled, a few bricks on the left wall show that only one tier had been filled and sealed. Tyng's remains were moved with the others to Sherburne Cemetery on Coburn Road. A few bones are held at the Littlefield Library.

An Eagle Scout, 1980. Scout Gary Constantine received a citation from Tyngsborough Historical Commission President Elizabeth Demas on December 18, 1980. Constantine earned his eagle badge for his work clearing the grounds and helping to erect a fence around the historic Gould Cemetery.

The Winslow Schoolhouse. The schoolhouse, which had rested in Tyngsborough center since 1792, was moved to Main Street in Dunstable just over the town line in 1973, when the Adams House was moved (p. 58). Restored to its original condition by the Tyngsborough-Dunstable Historical Society, it now serves as their meetinghouse.

The Bicentennial Committee, 1976. A few of the many committee members are shown here. From left to right are: (front row) Robert Waugh, Marion Nista Morrison, Pat Poulakos, Frances Gray, Martin Brick, and Elizabeth Hagan; (back row) Henry Norris, Sarah Stecchi, Christina Bell, Kay Hedlund, Emily Hagan, Jerome Goldhammer, and Ben MacDonald. Festivities in 1975 included a dinner dance, sing-a-long, parade, fashion show, bike rally, and country fair. In 1976, worship services, a tricentennial celebration of the Tyng Mansion, the Bicentennial Pageant Ball, a parade, and a fair were held, ending with a firemen's muster.

Six

Recreation: Sporting and Taking It Easy

The Tyngsborough Baseball Team, 1909. The game of baseball has been played in town since its introduction. The first organized team was managed by Horace Clarke in 1922. A few players of that team were Charlie Lorman, Arthur Cummings, Leo Pelletier, and Max Sherburne. "Uncle Toot" Wilkins later managed teams until his death in 1957.

A Swing at the Merrill House, August 22, 1905. Gail Whitney of Gorham, Maine, had her picture taken while taking a ride on the old swing "in the shade of the old apple tree." The Merrill House, different from the one mentioned on p. 59, stood on the site of the present Firehouse Restaurant. The caption reads: "How'd you like to spoon with me?"

The Bicycle Club. In the Gay '90s the sports of bicycling and roller skating gained popularity. Here, a bicycle club, perhaps from Lowell, spreads out across the side steps of the Willowdale Hotel.

Willowdale Park. Established in 1867, Willowdale was a popular tourist grove of residents and out-of-towners. Located on the eastern shore of Mascuppic Lake, it offered shaded pine groves, a fine beach, and many recreations. The area was so popular the Lowell trolley line extended a branch to the lake from Dracut.

The Willowdale Pavilion. Three bathers stand at the wharf before the turn of the century, while three men ready a boat farther up the shore. The pavilion, large and extravagant, could accommodate hundreds in its dance hall. It and many other buildings were totally destroyed by fire in 1897.

Bathers. This family from the east side of town is all set to go for a swim in 1912. Suits for the men were makeshift, while those for the women seemed like normal garb for the day. In those days few people were good swimmers, and a small swimming hole was preferred to open water.

The Steamer *Willowdale*. Plying the waters of Mascuppic, this steamer made frequent trips around the lake and to Mount Rock Park on the western shore. This steamer was originally called the *Vesper*, and it operated on the Merrimack River until it was moved to the lake in 1896.

The *Governor Allen*. Parked at the *Vesper* boat dock, the *Governor Allen* was one of the last to travel the river. It is shown here more favorably than in the photograph on p. 12. The smokestack on the roof was devised to lie down while passing under the bridge; when nearing it, a whistle blew, and the stack folded down with the pull of a rope.

The Wall at Colonial Hall. The stone wall has been replaced with Notre Dame's wrought iron fence. The sign on the gate here read: "Tis here I work & struggle hard to cure the sick and lame. Yet bye & bye of course I die yet they'll doctor just the same." Apt words for the gate of the sanitarium, which in those days meant a health spa.

Dr. Orrin Fitzgerald. When he bought the Brinley estate in 1890 (p. 35), health spas were the rage nationwide. It was a feather in any doctor's cap to have a retreat for the weary and feeble. But though his Colonial Hall began as such, it soon became noted as a get-away resort for the healthy and wealthy.

Senator Blackburn. Orrin Fitzgerald's prize racer is the subject of this drawing on the rear cover of his 1893 publicity pamphlet. The doctor's most valued possession, Senator Blackburn brought in much money over the years, and he was the foundation of the Colonial Hall Breeding Farm.

Independence Day, July 4, 1912. At a home once located off Coburn Road, a family sits down to dinner. The picture shows a closeness of family and an interest in celebrating our independence that is seldom seen in this day and age. The caption reads: "19 people, 2 dogs, 1 cat."

Harmony Grove. "Big George, 1898" is the caption of this photograph, taken at the popular grove along the river. On a heavy-duty seesaw, "Big George" clearly outweighs his wife and children. It looks as if there might have been a wager settled here. The buildings at the grove were destroyed by fire in 1900.

Fishing on the Merrimack, 1903. Three men are set to fish from atop a rock just north of the bridge. A fourth man in a boat behind them provides transport. Debris like this stump often appeared on the river's banks after spring floods.

An Automobile Carnival, 1909. When the sport was young, auto races were held on Pawtucket Boulevard and Sherburne Avenue between Tyngsborough Bridge and Townsend Avenue in Lowell. Racers entered town on the boulevard and returned by way of Sherburne. The hairpin turn on the next page was the site of many accidents.

Spectators at an Automobile Race. Star drivers like Barney Oldfield were a main draw at these races. Two men per car were required, a driver and a mechanic. The weight of the mechanic on the passenger side was helpful in the turns. Here Louis Strang with his Buick comes in for a win in 1909.

The Hairpin Turn. At the bridge, this was the turning point of the Merrimack Valley Race Course. Drivers raced around this corner, often on two wheels, and entered Sherburne Avenue (at the top of the photograph). The large oak tree was considered a peril to drivers who wanted it cut down to lessen the curve. The tree's removal was unannounced, creating an uproar among town residents.

The Genoa Club. This large clubhouse was another of many outing buildings to succumb to fire between 1895 and 1915. It was built on the east bank of the river at what was called Genoa Park, off present Phalanx Road, behind the Blue Moon on Frost Road.

The Chute, 1912. This toboggan chute at the Vesper Country Club offered a quick ride and maybe a rush of adrenaline. From the 30-foot tower, it was not impossible to be sent into the river. Cross-country skiing, and skating on flooded tennis courts, were also popular winter pastimes.

118

The Tyngsborough Country Club. Two men on the third green in the summer of 1932 are pictured is this 1934 advertisement for the country club. The ad reads: "One of the prettiest and golfiest 9-hole courses in New England. Par 35—always in the pink of condition." The course was built *c.* 1924 by Isaiah Spindell on what was once the Queen Farm.

Bath Time. There was little danger of a child getting in trouble in a small pot like this. One-year-old Juanita Sargent doesn't seem to mind the open air while cooling off on her grandparents' front lawn on Long Pond Road in 1926.

A Tyngsborough-Dunstable Clam Bake, 1921. This scene is only a small part of a large rolling photograph taken at the Martin Luther Grounds along the Merrimack River off Farwell Road. The image had been rolled up for many years and cracked when opened. Many familiar faces of the last generations of the1800s and the first ones of this century can be seen. Old-timers of both towns are listed, and some of the teenagers seen are still with us today. Most of the

Tyngsboro—Dunstable, Mass.
Martin Luthier Grounds

transportation to the grounds was provided by river steamer, but at these town outings the small dirt road known as River Road was often used, crossing the railroad tracks. This crossing amid the corn field was a dangerous one. In the 1930s, an entire musical band from Lowell was killed while crossing the tracks after their performance.

Willowdale. After the grand pavilion at Willowdale Park burned down in 1897, the groves quickly filled with summer camps, offering seasonal retreats for folks from as far away as Boston and New York. Many of these camps eventually became year-round dwellings. Lake Mascuppic, Althea Pond, Long Pond, Massapoag, Flint's Pond, and the Merrimack River were skirted by hundreds of such camps. By 1910, one-fifth of Tyngsborough's evaluation was in seasonal camps, bungalows, and cottages. In 1895, the population of the town was 652; the summertime population a decade later was twice that number.

Students on Flint's Pond. During a break in their studies, these six girls from Notre Dame Academy row about the pond that abuts the school property. Because most students also lived at the school, many activities and recreations were afforded them to fill the idle time when school was over.

A Sunday School Lawn Party, 1933. These girls stand ready for the Sunday parade in front of the carriage shed at the Evangelical church. With carriages and floats decorated, they are: Juanita Sargent, Marion Sherburne, Eleanor Parrish, Louise Clarke, and Margaret Coburn. The girl looking away is unidentified.

The Play *Better Times*. Under auspices of the PTA, a play entitled *Better Times* ran at the Tyngsborough Town Hall, on November 17 and 18, 1932. During the Depression, an acting troupe arrived in town from New York. The government-sponsored idea was to stage a play with local talent to lift the town's spirits during those dire times. The actors and other participants are, from left to right: (front row) Alice and Juliette Gaudette, Vera Bell, Pearly Knight,

Clarence Carkin, David Knight, Rita LeBlanc, Margaret Davis, Ernest Carkin, Harry Coles, George Robeson, and Norman Sherburne; (middle row) Jardine Davis, Madeline Dunning, Helen Woodward, Elizabeth Keyes, Frances Clarke, Myrla Wilbur, Jessie Algrove, Helen Bell, Bernice Sherburne, Nellie Pierce, and Ray Norton; (back row) Helen Brown, Francis Savill, Delma Brown, Dorothy Dunning, Miss Brown, and Mary Hayes.

Ice Hockey. George Ford and Joe Pelletier square off on the ice at Flint's Pond behind Ford's Turkey Farm on Flint Road. This lower part of the pond received less wind and provided better ice for skating. The Evangelical church can be seen in the background.

The Tyngsborough Playground. Anna Cobleigh seems to be watching over assorted children at the playground behind the church on Kendall Road. Mrs. George Woodsum and Mrs. Warren Riley began the Tyngsborough Co-operative Nursery School Association in 1956. The playground was built behind the Evangelical church, so preschool children could learn to interact with others.

The Village Players

PRESENT

"The Whole Town's Talking"

Tyngsborough Town Hall

Thursday and Friday, March 1 and 2, 1956

at 8 o'clock

CAST

HENRY SIMMONS, a manufacturer	RICHARD STARKEY
HARRIET SIMMONS, his wife	HAZEL INCH
ETHEL SIMMONS, their daughter	JANICE COBLEIGH
CHESTER BINNEY, Simmon's partner	FRANK COBLEIGH, Jr.
LETTY LYTHE, a motion picture star	BARBARA ROBINSON
DONALD SWIFT, a motion picture director . .	RICHARD FAY
ROGER SHIELDS, of Chicgo's smart set	FRANK PARKER
LILA WILSON ⎫ friends of Ethel	SUSAN LUSTIG
SALLY OTIS ⎭	CAROL HATFIELD
ANNIE, the maid	JOAN LANTRY
SADIE BLOOM	MABEL CARKIN

TIME:- Early Summer

PLACE:- The Simmon's Home, Sandusky, Ohio

Stage—Frances Gray   *Director*—George Bell
        Frank Cobleigh, Jr.   *Prompter*—Mrs. Richard Starkey

Fair Committees

Mr. Charles Derbabian
Mrs. Ethel Sargent
Mr. Frank Herrmann
Mrs. Frank Herrmann
Mr. Martin Brick
Mrs. Martin Brick

SALES TABLES

FANCY WORK TABLE	CHILDREN'S TABLE
Bernice Sherburne	Charlotte Stone
Mabel Sherburne	Daisy Wilkins
FLOWER TABLE	CANDY TABLE
Maud Currier	Ethel Sargent
Edith Holdsworth	Angelia Starkey

NOVELTY and GRAB TABLE
Tyra Allgrove
Nellie Moore

FARMERS TABLE

A Village Improvement Association Play, 1956. The VIA presented a play nearly every year at the Town Hall in addition to a supper and fair. Money was used to fund association projects, such as building Butterfield Road in 1897 and sidewalks in 1915. The VIA, established in 1895, had its beginnings with the Tree Society in 1844. The last meeting was in 1959.

Acknowledgments

If not for the generous help of many people who now live, or have lived, in town, this book would never have gotten off the ground. The many scenes pictured in Village Improvement Association annuals provided a good starting point. The Tyngsborough Historical Commission and the folks at the Littlefield Library were ever-ready to offer photographs and information.

For the lending of excellent photographs from their collections, I would like to thank Ruth and Alvin Choate, Barbara Magoon, and Christina and George Bell. Also invaluable were the collections of the late Clara Marshall, Lillian Choate, Charles Derbabian, Chester Queen, and Francis Gray.

Of course, photographs without captions are only half as good, and there are many who went out of their way in offering names, dates, and other particulars. In addition to the above mentioned they are: Joe Pelletier, Louise Lorman, Dick Choate, Ramona Jordan, Dennis LeBlanc, Sandy Kelly, Carl Gray, Blanche Clarke, Charles Chronopoulos, Bob Waugh, Avis and George Tilton, Dick Lustig, Rita and Frank Cobleigh, Doris Bergeron, Carol Britain, Carol Butt, Arthur Constantine, Reggie Dove, Guy Constantine, Carol Bacon, Francis May, Stella Beh, Harold Bell Jr., Bob Gray, and my mother Juanita Morton.

Lastly, many thanks to Tyngsborough-Dunstable Historical Society President Richard Provencher for suggesting that I begin this project.